Reading Magazine

Year 3

Reading Magazine Year 3
NAPLAN*-Format Practice Tests

CIRCUS

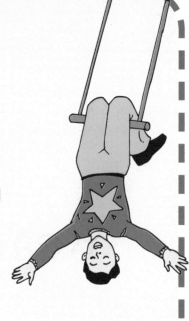

Peter and Jasmine were at the circus with their parents. They liked the different things to see.

'I want to see the clowns,' said Peter. 'They make me laugh with their funny hair.'

'I want to see the elephants as well,' said Jasmine.
'The ponies are next to the elephant tent as well so we can see two things.'

'You will get to see all the special things the circus has,' said the children's father, 'we will be here all day.'

'Great,' replied the two children together.

Making Pancakes

Things you need

- 2 cups plain flour
- 3 teaspoons baking powder
- 2 tablespoons castor sugar
- 2 eggs, lightly beaten
- 750ml buttermilk
- 75g unsalted butter, melted

How to make pancakes

Stir the flour, baking powder and sugar together in a bowl.

Add the eggs, buttermilk and melted butter, mix it all.

Ask an adult to heat a non stick frypan for you.

Pour some of the pancake batter into the pan and cook for 2-3 minutes until bubbles appear on the surface.

Turn the pancake over gently and cook for another minute.

Enjoy!

© Alfred Fletcher
Coroneos Publications

Reading Magazine Year 3
NAPLAN*-Format Practice Tests

CHINESE NEW YEAR

Chinese New Year is the most important celebration in the Chinese year.

It begins on the first day of the Chinese calendar, which usually is in February. The fun continues for fifteen days.

In Chinese New Year celebrations, people wear red clothes; give children 'lucky money' in red envelopes for luck. Family members gather at each other's homes for special meals.

Chinese New Year ends with the lantern festival, where people hang decorated lanterns in temples and carry lanterns in a parade under the full moon. The highlight of the lantern festival is the dragon dance. In Australia Chinese New Year is not an official holiday but many people make it a holiday.

新年快乐

REPTILES

Reptiles, are air-breathing, generally "cold-blooded" animals whose skin is usually covered in scales. They generally have four limbs, except snakes, and lay eggs. The first reptiles were the dinosaurs which once ruled the earth.

Modern reptiles inhabit every continent with the exception of Antarctica, and four living types are currently known. They are the crocodiles and alligators, tuataras, snakes and lizards and turtles and tortoises. Their are over eight thousand different types of reptiles.

The majority of reptile species are egg-laying, although some species of lizards are capable of giving live birth. Reptiles range in size from tiny geckos that grow to only 1.6 cm to the saltwater crocodile that reaches 6 metres in length and weighs over 1,000 kg. The study of reptiles is called herpetology.

© Alfred Fletcher
Coroneos Publications

Reading Magazine Year 3
NAPLAN*-Format Practice Tests

Being a Vegetarian

A vegetarian has a plant-based diet including fruits, vegetables, cereal grains, nuts, and seeds. Some vegetarians eat dairy products and eggs. A vegetarian does not eat meat, including: red meat, game, poultry, fish, shellfish, and animal products.

Sally is a vegetarian and she says "Being a vegetarian means I save animals and help the environment."

Some vegetarians like Skye do not even eat eggs and honey because they come from animals.

"I can't eat any animal products as they make me feel sick," said Skye. "Some of my friends do but my health is too important to me."

People have lots of reasons for not eating meat and some of these are religious and cultural. For example many people of the Hindu religion are vegetarian.

Naveen tells us, "My family's religion is Hinduism and so have a vegetarian diet."
People have lots of reasons for not eating meat and some of these are religious and cultural. For example many people of the Hindu religion are vegetarian.

THE ADVENTURES OF DELPHI

(an extract from a novel by May Watson)

Delphi's eyes followed the humanoid figure that was trying to capture her. She knew she should not have wandered into the castle perimeter but she had never seen anything like it and was curious. The aliens in the castle controlled the whole country now and they had transformed it into something very strange.

The old stone walls she was now backed into were covered in coloured thin metallic ropes that went into large silver boxes which gave off strange sounds. She could see four of them from her position as she tried to slide along the wall nearer to the drawbridge. The drawbridge was her only hope of escape and the way back to her little village of Mogra.

Delphi knew that the figure before her was not really a person but one of the slaves of the aliens which they made in the old dungeons. Still she thought they were dangerous as they had come to her village and taken old Samuel away. She was scared of it but still wanted to escape.

The humanoid lunged at her but it was slower than the thin little girl and Delphi ducked past its arms. She bolted for the lowered drawbridge and was nearly out when she ran into one of the iron horses they used to move around in.

Dogs

Dogs have been called 'man's best friend' because they are faithful and loyal to their owners. Dogs and people have been together for centuries as dogs help people. They do jobs like helping guard houses, herd sheep and cattle and they even do rescues and work with police.

Dogs make great pets because they like being with families. You know when a dog is friendly because its tail wags up and down. You can always pat a dog but never pull its tail

Korea: A Divided Country

Korea is a country divided into two states North Korea and South. Before 1948 Korea was one country. Located in Asia it borders China , Russia and is separated from Japan by the Korea Strait.

The combined population of the Koreans is about 73 million (North Korea: 23 million, South Korea: 50 million). Korea is chiefly populated by the Korean people but there are also some Chinese and Japanese people who live there.

Korean is the official language of both North and South Korea.

The Zoo

Cedric went to the zoo for his birthday with his parents and best friend, Colin. At the zoo they walked around the Reptile House first. Here they saw snakes, tortoises and the giant Komodo Dragon. After this they saw all the Australian animals such as kangaroos, wombats, wallabies and koalas.

After a lunch of delicious fish and chips and juice the four of them had an elephant ride. It swayed and rocked but they felt safe. Later they saw the huge rhinoceros and tall giraffe. The best part of the day for Cedric was the crocodiles as they were being fed fish and he saw their sharp teeth. After that they left for dinner at Yummo's Restaurant.

Multicultural Day

Sofia Primary School recently had a multicultural day to celebrate Harmony Week and they asked students what they thought of the experience they had on the day. Below are some student comments written in class.

Daisha: I loved multicultural day because of the food my friends brought from home. Sofia had some dolmades and Luigi had pepperoni pizza.

Carmel: I enjoyed the dancing. We had a Scottish dance group come in and one man played the bagpipes. It was the best.

Kim: All of us shared food on the picnic lunch. The teachers even brought dishes from their countries. Mrs Krakow brought three giant homemade Polish salamis and shared them.

Aboriginal Myth

One of the most important Aboriginal myths is about the Rainbow Serpent. This story is told by many tribes all over Australia. These stories are part of Dreamtime Myths that are part of Aboriginal culture. These Dreaming stories tell about the patterns of life.

This Rainbow Serpent is a snake of enormous size that lived in the deepest waterholes and comes from the stars. It shows itself as a rainbow to people who never see its real shape.

The Rainbow Serpent moves about in the water and rain and changes the land into different shapes. It also interacts with people and can give them blessings or make them sick. The Rainbow Serpent can move across all of Australia and is said to control water by making rivers and gullies.

The Aboriginal people also paint the Rainbow Serpent on rocks and bark as part of their art. Dreamtime stories are also told in song and dance and modern Aboriginal artists use these stories to paint on canvas. This is important because Aboriginal history is oral. They didn't write their stories down but rather told them. These stories were passed down through the generations.

Escape from the Fifth Moon
(extract from a novel by Hannah May)

They turned their moon-bikes around to look at the dust in the distance from their pursuers. Andy and Harley then put their heads down and headed for the cover of the tunnels. Harley followed her knowing that they only had about one orbihour before they were caught. The moon dust and debris billowed behind the bikes as they raced across the dry landscape covering them in the sandy coloured dust.

The tunnels could be there only hope of escape from the following Akroins who wanted Andy. She was the only weapon that could defeat them and her ability to see the future was essential in the moon wars. The tunnels of the Isikarma, the native people of the fifth moon, also held dangers for outsiders. There were tales of people entering the tunnels and never being seen again. Harley knew they had to take that chance.

Andy raced her bike into the first of five tunnel entrances they saw and only slowed as the darkness enveloped them. She flicked her bikes lights on and continued slowly while Harley followed her. They went on like this for two orbihours before they saw signs of Isikarma life. Harley gestured to her that they should turn their moon-bikes off. As they did Harley and Andy saw the three eyes of an Isikarma peering at them from a doorway.

Lions

The lion is the second-largest big cat. Lions are found in Africa and Asia. Lions live for 10–14 years in the wild, while in captivity they can last 20 years. They often live in grassland.

A pride of lions consists of females and young and a small number of males. Groups of females typically hunt together, mostly on antelope. Lions have been a species sought for show in zoos. The male lion is easily recognized by its mane.

Day at the Park

"Let's go to the park and ride on the merry-go-round," called Ben to his sister Tiffany.

"Only if I can have a turn on the monkey bars and swings too," she said.

"I'll ask mum," said Ben. "I think she will agree if we say we'll be home by five."

"Fabulous," Tiffany shouted as she raced to the back door.

© Alfred Fletcher
Coroneos Publications

Reading Magazine Year 3
NAPLAN*-Format Practice Tests

Stamp Collecting

Stamp collecting is the collecting of postage stamps. It is one of the world's most popular hobbies, with collectors in every country of the world. Many collectors enjoy finding and keeping stamps without worrying about the story behind them. A large collection will require some knowledge and people who study stamps are called philatelists.

The first postage stamp in the world was the Penny Black which was issued in Britain in 1840. Since then people have been collecting stamps although the hobby began with children. Some stamps are valuable and people collect stamps for money.

You can collect stamps by getting them off envelopes. To do this you get some warm water and place the stamp and envelope in the water. The glue on the stamp softens and you can peel it off. Dry it on a paper towel and you are a collector!

Anzac Day

Anzac Day is a national day of remembrance in Australia and New Zealand, and is commemorated by both countries on the twenty-fifth of April every year to remember soldiers of the Australian and New Zealand Army Corps (ANZAC) who fought at Gallipoli in Turkey during World War I. The word ANZAC stands for Australian and New Zealand Army Corps.

These days Anzac Day is a day we remember those who fought in all wars and most towns have a memorial service to honour men and women from those towns that have died in wars. In a big city marches are held through the streets very early in the morning after a Dawn Service where a wreath is laid. It is a very important day for all Australians but also those from New Zealand.

Anzac Day is celebrated by Australians all over the world and also in Turkey where the fighting took place. Schools celebrate Anzac Day as a special event and many have assemblies to tell students about the history of the day.

General Birdwood at Entrance to Shrap

Kangaroos

A kangaroo is a marsupial and they live all over Australia. Larger kangaroos have adapted well to human habitation and most species are quite common. The kangaroo is very important to Australians as it is our national symbol and its picture is on the countries coat-of-arms with the emu. It is also pictured on some of our money.

The word kangaroo is taken from an aboriginal word 'gangurru' and Captain James Cook was the first explorer to record the name. The early settlers thought kangaroos very strange animals and were popular in zoos both dead and alive. Male kangaroos are called bucks and the females, jills. The young are called joeys and live in a pouch. The common term for kangaroos is a 'roo' while a group is called a mob.

There are four main species of kangaroos, the Red, the Eastern Grey, the Western Grey and the Antilopine Kangaroo. None of these species are in any danger but some smaller species are becoming rarer. They eat grasses and shrubs and have few predators such as eagles, dingoes and goannas.

The kangaroo was very important to the aborigines because of its fur and food qualities. The kangaroo is an important Australian animal and is part of our history.

© Alfred Fletcher
Coroneos Publications

Reading Magazine Year 3
NAPLAN*-Format Practice Tests

The Horseman of Dry Creek

(extract from a novel by Bill Russell)

Abe Finchcombe had always lived on the ranch at Dry Creek and had done since he was born there twenty-two years before. He had grown up on the ranch working beside his father and they had the best horses in the county. Abe was famous for his knowledge and skill with horses and could train them to do anything.

Today was the day he was going to begin to teach a young wild horse how to take a saddle. Everything was ready in the yard and the black, bright eyed animal waited for him with jittery legs. Abe's dad warned him to be careful as the horse was full of life and strong. The ranch hands had gathered to watch the outcome with some men thinking this horse might win.

The rangy beast circled around the old wooden yard kicking up blasts of dust with its hooves. Its eyes looked wild and it began to kick its legs as Abe walked into the yard with a lead. Talking soothingly to the horse he allowed it to run around the yard until it released all its nervous energy. All the time he moved closer and closer to its now sweaty body. He began to run his hand along its side and then slipped the lead over its head.

The horse ran and he let the rope slip through his gloved hand until the lead was at its full extent. Then he began to draw the horse toward him and it came. He rubbed his hand on its nose to calm it and them he began to lead it around. One man whistled in admiration at his ability.

© Alfred Fletcher
Coroneos Publications

Reading Magazine Year 3
NAPLAN*-Format Practice Tests

Read the following story and answer the four questions below.

The Ant and the Grasshopper

In a field one summer's day a Grasshopper was hopping about, chirping and singing to its heart's content. An Ant passed by, bearing along with great toil a grain of corn he was taking to the ant nest.

"Why not come and chat with me," said the Grasshopper, "instead of working in that way?"

"I am helping to lay up food for the winter," said the Ant, "and recommend you to do the same."

"Why bother about winter?" said the Grasshopper; we have got plenty of food at present."

But the Ant went on its way and continued its work.

When the winter came the Grasshopper had no food and found itself dying of hunger, while it saw the ants distributing every day corn and grain from the stores they had collected in the summer.

Then the Grasshopper knew: It is best to prepare for the days of necessity.

Questions

1   **The characters in the story are?**
   - the grasshopper
   - the ant
   - the ant and the grasshopper
   - the corn

2   **Which sentence is true?**
   - the grasshopper is hard working
   - the grasshopper is ready for winter
   - the ant is taking it easy in summer
   - the ant is hard working

3   **The phrase 'bearing along with great toil' means?**
   - working very hard
   - resting in a grassy spot
   - stopping and having a chat
   - the grasshopper likes work

4   **Write the numbers 1 to 4 in the spaces to show the events of the story in order**
   - _____ the ant continues to work
   - _____ the ants distribute food
   - _____ the grasshopper is hopping about and singing
   - _____ the grasshopper is not worried about winter

READING MAGAZINE YEAR 3 is a supplement to

YEAR 3 READING
NAPLAN*-FORMAT PRACTICE TESTS with answers
© Alfred Fletcher 2010
Published by Coroneos Publications 2010
ISBN 978-1-921565-47-2

YEAR 3

READING

NAPLAN*- FORMAT PRACTICE TESTS
with answers

Essential preparation for Year 3
NAPLAN* Tests in Reading

ALFRED FLETCHER

CORONEOS PUBLICATIONS

YEAR 3 READING
NAPLAN*- FORMAT PRACTICE TESTS with answers
© Alfred Fletcher 2010
Published by Coroneos Publications 2010

ISBN 978-1-921565-47-2

* These tests have been produced by Coroneos Publications independently of Australian governments and are not officially endorsed publications of the NAPLAN program

THIS BOOK IS AVAILABLE FROM RECOGNISED BOOKSELLERS OR CONTACT:

Coroneos Publications
Telephone: (02) 9624 3 977   Facsimile: (02) 9624 3717
Business Address: 6/195 Prospect Highway Seven Hills 2147
Postal Address: PO Box 2 Seven Hills 2147
Website: www. coroneos.com.au or www.basicskillsseries.com
E-mail: coroneospublications@westnet.com.au

Contents

NOTE:

• Students have 45 minutes to complete a test.

• Students must use 2B or HB pencils only.

The NAPLAN* Test

NAPLAN* is an acronym representing the **National Assessment Program for Literacy and Numeracy.** The tests are conducted in May each year to determine the Literacy and Numeracy skills of students in Australian schools. Controversially, the results have been used by the authorities to benchmark schools on the distribution of these skills amongst students of those schools.

The tests are conducted in Year 3, Year 5, Year 7 and Year 9. The assessment program involves students completing four separate tests, in four timed minute sessions.

The separate tests are:

· Writing: Students write a narrative in a 40 minute session.

· Reading: Each student is given a 6 or 12 page stimulus book and completes a test comprising 35 to 40 plus multiple choice questions.

· Language Conventions: This is a test of spelling, grammar and sentence structure.

· Numeracy : A test consisting of multiple choice or short answer questions in numeracy (mathematics). In year 7 and Year 9 students answer **non-calculator** and **calculator allowed** questions in separate parts of the test.

This book is designed to help you practise for the the NAPLAN* tests and develop the skills necessary to competently handle any task presented to you at this stage of your development.

* The practice tests in this book have been produced by Five Senses Education Pty Ltd

   independently of Australian governments and are not officially endorsed publications of the

   NAPLAN program

The Reading Task

This book is designed to help you practise for the Reading section of the NAPLAN* test and develop the skills necessary to competently handle any reading task presented to you at this stage of your development. The NAPLAN* test in reading examines your ability to read texts and understand what you have read. Practicing these will develop skills that will assist you in all areas of your reading and comprehension.

Also included in this book are some hints on how to improve your reading and comprehension skills. Follow these hints and use them in your work as they may assist you in gaining additional vital marks under examination conditions. They will also help you develop your overall English skills and benefit your work in general.

We wish you all the best for the exam and know that the activities and tasks in this book will assist you in reaching your reading potential.

The NAPLAN* test includes a reading task which asks you to read a variety of texts that are similar to the things you read in the classroom. These texts are in the form of a 'Reading Magazine' which usually contains, in Year 3 SIX pages of texts that you will have to read and understand. This magazine is TWELVE pages long by Year Nine. There is also a title page and a back page which has the sample text on it. This last page is not part of the exam. This magazine is in colour and the graphics or pictures can help you understand the story. No questions are asked specifically on the graphics.

The other section of the reading task is a booklet of questions that asks you about each of the six texts you have read in the 'Reading Magazine'. These questions test your ability to understand and comprehend what you have read. You have to 'shade the bubble' to record your answer although in some questions you are asked to number the boxes to show the order of events in the text. Sample questions are provided at the end of this section to give an indication of the type of questions that you might encounter in this book and in the test.

What Markers Look For When Examining Your Work

Of course your test will be marked and so it is good to know what the examiner or marker is looking for. The examiner is looking to test your ability to read different types of texts such as factual texts, stories and as you get older things like letters, posters, poetry and reviews. All the questions are based on the work you have been doing in class and there is no penalty for incorrect answers. The difficulty of the questions will vary from straightforward comprehension to more complex understanding and comparative questions.

Each year the examination tests the skill and developmental areas appropriate to the level being tested. In Year 5 for example the test might, in one year, test your ability to find information, connect ideas, come to conclusions, find the main purpose of a text, compare differing points of view and show your understanding of a character, what they do and why they do it.

In some ways the reading test is also a test of vocabulary and how well you know complex vocabulary and are able to interpret it. I cannot emphasise enough the worth of developing a good vocabulary as it will help you in all areas of every subject that you will be asked to do during your education.

The reading section is reported similarly to the other areas, that is, in bands with Band 10 being the highest in Year Nine, Band 9 in Year 7, Band 8 in Year 5 and Band 6 in Year 3. Similarly the bottom Bands change according to Year with Band 1 the lowest skill level in Year 3.

In this section you do not have to write sentence responses just shade bubbles or write numbers. You will be expected to answer all the questions and select one bubble from the four choices (usually) provided in the question. If you make a mistake put a X through the bubble and shade the bubble you now think the answer should be.

By understanding clearly the information you have just read you will have taken the first major step on your path to success in these tests. By knowing what you have to do you will be prepared for it and confident in what you need to do to succeed. Re-read these introductory notes several times. Then you know what to expect in the exam and won't be surprised by the words in the exam or the format. Practice questions such as those in this book make you familiar with the language and format of the paper. The next section gives you some reading and comprehension tips to help improve your ability to reach your potential in the exam.

IMPROVING YOUR READING AND COMPREHENSION SKILLS

Reading improvement is a matter of practice and developing your skills and understanding so you can comprehend the text(s) you are reading. There are some simple things you can do to build your skills in this area.

Read as Widely as You Can and With Purpose

The best way to improve your reading skills is to read. This doesn't have to be books but might be magazines, newspapers, pamphlets, anything really that will develop your ability to learn words. As you read you will meet words that you don't know – this is a great opportunity to grab a dictionary or ask someone what that word means and add it to your vocabulary. The wider your vocabulary the better your understanding will be and you can then read more difficult texts. Vocabulary is one of the keys to understanding. Use a library for free reading materials.

Read Different Text Types

By reading and knowing the different text types you will be more confident when going into any activity in any subject, not just the exam. Try to read more than narrative texts try reading recounts, expositions, procedures, descriptions and discussions for example. As you get older you will read poetry, biography and reviews as well. Try and read for at least 20 minutes a day and more as you get older.

Learn Simple Literary Devices

As you get older you will need to recognise more than paragraphs, sentences and the simple parts of sentences. As you read you will be required to recognise and understand simple literary devices such as similes and synonyms and be able to understand why they are used. As a reader you will also be asked to understand the different levels of meaning in a text (literal, inferential and evaluative).

Develop Your Skills through Practise and Repetition

You have already taken one step by reading this book. To be a higher order reader you need to be able to predict in your reading and be able to identify and discuss different text types and identify bias and point of view in a text. One of the final stages is to be able to question or even challenge what the writer is saying after reflecting on the material. To be able to do these things you need to practise your skills at different levels.

The secret here is to keep testing yourself on harder texts and question types once you have mastered the level you are on. Don't push yourself harder than this. There is no point going to the next level if you haven't understood all the reading at the level you are on. Reading without comprehending what you are reading is frustrating. Go back and gain confidence with what you can do.

Now it is time to try some questions and see how you go.

SAMPLE QUESTIONS

Read the following story and answer the four questions on the next page. You will find these questions similar to the types you will find in this book and the examination.

The Ant and the Grasshopper

In a field one summer's day a Grasshopper was hopping about, chirping and singing to its heart's content. An Ant passed by, bearing along with great toil a grain of corn he was taking to the ant nest.

"Why not come and chat with me," said the Grasshopper, "instead of working in that way?"

"I am helping to lay up food for the winter," said the Ant, "and recommend you to do the same."

"Why bother about winter?" said the Grasshopper; we have plenty of food at present."

But the Ant went on its way and continued its work. When the winter came the Grasshopper had no food and found itself dying of hunger, while it saw the ants distributing every day corn and grain from the stores they had collected in the summer.

Then the Grasshopper knew: It is best to prepare for the days of necessity.

1 **The characters in the story are?**

- ○ the grasshopper
- ○ the ant
- ○ the ant and the grasshopper
- ○ the corn

Shade one bubble

2 **Which sentence is true?**

- ○ the grasshopper is hard working
- ○ the grasshopper is ready for winter
- ○ the ant is taking it easy in summer
- ○ the ant is hard working

3 **The phrase 'bearing along with great toil' means?**

- ○ working very hard
- ○ resting in a grassy spot
- ○ stopping and having a chat
- ○ the grasshopper likes work

4 **Write the numbers 1 to 4 in the spaces to show the events of the story in order**

____ the ant continues to work

____ the ants distribute food

____ the grasshopper is hopping about and singing

____ the grasshopper is not worried about winter

End of Sample Questions.

To complete the rest of the questions in this book you will need to refer to the *Year 3 Naplan*Format Reading Booklet*

READING TEST 1

Read the story about the *Circus* on page 2 of the reading booklet and answer the following questions.

1   The names of the two children in the story are?   Shade one bubble

○ Peter and Paul

○ Jasmine and Father

○ Peter and Jasmine

○ Peter and Father

2   Which sentence is correct?

○ The children have all day at the circus

○ The children are at the circus alone

○ Peter and Jasmine like lions

○ The children are afraid of clowns

3   Peter wants to see?

○ elephants

○ clowns

○ ponies

○ tents

4   What animal is near the elephants?

○ tigers

○ lions

○ giraffes

○ ponies

5   **What word in the story tells us the children are pleased to be at the circus?**

○ see

○ great

○ different

○ make

6   **Another good title for this story could be**

○ Parents at the Circus

○ Circus Life

○ Animal Fun

○ A Day at the Circus

Read the story about *Making Pancakes* on page 3 of the reading booklet and answer the following questions

7   **Two ingredients of pancakes are?**

○ flour and water

○ flour and salt

○ flour and butter

○ eggs and water

8   **What do you need 3 teaspoons of to make pancakes?**

○ castor sugar

○ baking powder

○ buttermilk

○ flour

9   How long do you cook the second side of a pancake for?

   ⭘ 1 minute

   ⭘ 2 minutes

   ⭘ 3 minutes

   ⭘ 4 minutes

10 The words under *Things you need* are written as a?

   ⭘ paragraph

   ⭘ booklet

   ⭘ list

   ⭘ memo

11 The word *beaten* in the recipe can also mean?

   ⭘ mixed

   ⭘ cooked

   ⭘ bashed

   ⭘ separate

12 Which word is NOT an instruction for the recipe?

   ⭘ stir

   ⭘ mix

   ⭘ enjoy

   ⭘ cook

Read the story about *Chinese New Year* on page 4 of the reading booklet and answer the following questions

13. Chinese New Year is usually in?

○ January

○ February

○ March

○ September

14 The colour red is used to?

○ decorate lanterns

○ paint dragon

○ show it is a holiday

○ scare off bad luck

15 Chinese New Year ends with?

○ dragon dance

○ lucky money

○ special meals

○ lantern festival

16 Which is true?

○ Chinese New Year is only celebrated in China.

○ Chinese New Year is an official holiday in Australia

○ Chinese New Year is a week long celebration

○ Chinese New Year is not an official holiday in Australia

17 The word *special* in the story could also mean?

○ bad

○ memorable

○ happy

○ useful

18 The word festival means?

○ carnival

○ outing

○ party

○ outing

Read the story about *Reptiles* on page 5 of the reading booklet and answer the following questions

19 Reptiles are covered in?

○ fur

○ skin

○ hair

○ scales

20 Most reptiles give birth by?

○ cloning

○ laying eggs

○ birth

○ reproduction

21 Which of the following is not a reptile?

○ snake

○ dinosaur

○ tuatara

○ frog

22 All reptiles have which qualities?

○ cold blooded and extinct

○ cold blooded and large

○ egg laying and four legged

○ scaly and cold blooded

23 The word *modern* in the passage is closest in meaning to?

○ stylish

○ current

○ slow

○ extinct

24 The smallest reptile is the?

○ crocodile

○ snake

○ lizard

○ gecko

25 The phrase reptiles inhabit every continent with the exception of

Antarctica means?

  ◯ they only live in Antarctica

  ◯ they live in Antarctica and Europe

  ◯ they live in the rest of the world but not Antarctica

  ◯ they don't live in Antarctica and Australia

Read the story about *Being a Vegetarian* on page 6 of the reading booklet and answer the following questions

26 Vegetarians can eat?

  ◯ fruits, vegetables and game

  ◯ fruits, vegetables and nuts

  ◯ nuts, eggs and poultry

  ◯ vegetables, nuts and eggs

27 Sally is a vegetarian because?

  ◯ she is a Hindu and wants to help the environment

  ◯ she wants to save animals and loves eggs

  ◯ she wants to help the environment and save animals

  ◯ she wants to become more tolerant to meats

28 Skye doesn't eat eggs and honey because?

○ they make her angry

○ they come from animals

○ hey do not mix together

○ she loves animals

29 Naveen is a vegetarian because of his?

○ name

○ school

○ race

○ religion

30 Another word for *important* in the passage might be?

○ relevant

○ necessary

○ excellent

○ trivial

31 Another title for this story might be ?

○ No Animal Products

○ Why I'm a Vegetarian

○ Religious Issues and Food

○ Meat is Bad

Read the story about *The Adventures of Delphi* on page 7 of the reading booklet and answer the following questions

32 Delphi wanders into the castle because she was?

○ young

○ lost

○ strange

○ curious

33 The story takes place in a

○ village

○ alien ship

○ castle

○ road

34 How many large silver boxes can Delphi see?

○ one

○ two

○ three

○ four

35 The castle walls are made of?

○ stone

○ metal

○ iron

○ rope

36 Another word for *'scared'* in the passage might be?

○ happy

○ frightened

○ tire

○ brave

37 The humanoid looks most like a ?

○ horse

○ Delphi

○ silver box

○ person

38 Write the numbers 1 to 4 in the spaces to show the order events happen in the story

_____ Delphi slides along the wall

_____ Delphi runs for the drawbridge

_____ Delphi wanders into the castle

_____ Delphi runs into the iron horse

END OF READING TEST 1

READING TEST 2

Read the story about *Dogs* on page 8 of the reading booklet and answer the following questions

1 Dogs are?

- ○ faithful and happy
- ○ happy and loyal
- ○ hairy and loyal
- ○ faithful and loyal

2 Which sentence is true?

- ○ Dogs have recently been made pets
- ○ Dogs have been with people for a year
- ○ Dogs have been with people for centuries
- ○ Dogs only work with the police

3 What jobs do dogs help people with?

- ○ guarding, herding and rescue
- ○ herding, rescue and shopping
- ○ guarding, teaching and rescue
- ○ rescue, police work and sniffing

4 Dogs like being with?

- ○ pets
- ○ cattle
- ○ dogs
- ○ families

5 **What should you never do to a dog?**

○ pat the dog gently

○ feed the dog

○ cuddle the dog

○ pull the tail of the dog

6 **Another good title for this story could be?**

○ Man's Best Friend

○ Dog Jobs

○ Dog People

○ A Day With a Dog

Read the story about *Korea* on page 9 of the reading booklet and answer the following questions

7 **Korea is divided into how many states?**

○ one

○ two

○ three

○ four

8 **How many people live in South Korea?**

○ 25 million

○ 35 million

○ 50 million

○ 75 million

9 **What two other kinds of people live in Korea?**

  ○ Russian and Japanese

  ○ Chinese and Japanese

  ○ Chinese and Russian

  ○ Korean and Chinese

10 **The word *combined* can also mean?**

  ○ detached

  ○ joined

  ○ nailed

  ○ coped

11 **The word *divided* can also mean?**

  ○ zero

  ○ multiply

  ○ couple

  ○ separate

12 **Which countries are joined to Korea by land?**

  ○ Russia and China

  ○ China and Japan

  ○ Russia and Japan

  ○ Japan and North Korea

Read the story about *The Zoo* on page 10 of the reading booklet and answer the following questions

13 How many people went to the zoo ?

○ one

○ two

○ three

○ four

14 The first animals they saw were the?

○ kangaroos

○ reptiles

○ giraffes

○ elephants

15 The last animal they saw was the?

○ elephant

○ wombat

○ giraffe

○ crocodile

16 Which is true?

○ Cedric thought the best part of the day was seeing crocodiles

○ Cedric thought the best part of the day was seeing Colin

○ Cedric thought the best part of the day was visiting Yummo's

○ Cedric thought the best part of the day was eating lunch

17 The word *delicious* in the story could also mean?

○ good

○ tasty

○ delicate

○ unpleasant

18 The word *swayed* means?

○ to move up and down

○ to move backwards

○ to move from side to side

○ to move down

Read the story about *Multicultural Day* on page 11 of the reading booklet and answer the following questions

19 Multicultural day is celebrated in?

○ Multicultural Week

○ Harmony Week

○ Multicultural Week

○ Harmony Day

20 Daisha loved the day because of the?

○ salami

○ dancing

○ food

○ picnic

21 **Which student brought the pizza to school?**

○ Sofia

○ Carmel

○ Kim

○ Luigi

22 **What word tells us the Polish salami was cooked at Mrs Krakow's place?**

○ fresh

○ delicious

○ homemade

○ giant

23 **The word *experience* in the passage is closest in meaning to?**

○ trip

○ participation

○ observe

○ allowed

24 **How many giant salamis were at the picnic?**

○ one

○ two

○ three

○ four

25 The phrase *'It was the best'* means?

- ○ Carmel enjoyed the food
- ○ Carmel enjoyed the dancing
- ○ Carmel danced well
- ○ Carmel had a bad day

Read the story about *Aboriginal Myth* on page 12 of the reading booklet and answer the following questions

26 Dreaming stories tell about?

- ○ animals
- ○ landscape
- ○ patterns of life
- ○ art and painting

27 The Rainbow Serpent appears as a?

- ○ waterhole
- ○ landscape
- ○ snake
- ○ rainbow

28 How did the Aborigines pass down their stories?

- ○ in books
- ○ orally
- ○ dance
- ○ runes

29 The Rainbow Serpent lives in?

○ waterholes

○ rivers

○ the landscape

○ deepest waterholes

30 Another word for *enormous* in the passage might be?

○ insignificant

○ big

○ total

○ gigantic

31 How does the Rainbow Serpent interact with people?

○ it creates fear and art

○ it gives blessings and art

○ it gives blessings and sickness

○ it gives sickness and rivers

Read the story about *Escape from the Fifth Moon* on page 13 of the reading booklet and answer the following questions

32 Andy and Harley are running from the?

○ Isikarma

○ Akroins

○ Orbihours

○ Tunnels

33 **The landscape of the fifth moon is?**

○ wet and sandy

○ sandy and rocky

○ wet and rocky

○ sandy and dry

34 *'They'* **in the first line refers to?**

○ Akroins and Isikarma

○ Harley and Andy

○ Harley and Isikarma

○ Andy and Isikarma

35 **Why do the Akroins want Andy?**

○ she was very clever at war

○ she could defeat them

○ she and Harley were good fighters

○ she was a warrior

36 **Another word for *essential* in the passage might be?**

○ probable

○ minor

○ ability

○ necessary

37 The phrase *'as the darkness enveloped them'* means?

○ the darkness was lit by their lights

○ the darkness was all around them

○ the darkness was like a letter

○ the darkness was helped by stars

38 Write the numbers 1 to 4 in the spaces to show the order events happen in the story

_____ Andy and Harley saw the eyes of an Isikarma

_____ Andy and Harley head into the tunnels

_____ Andy and Harley turn to look at their pursuers

_____ Andy and Harley drive further into the tunnels

END OF READING TEST 2

READING TEST 3

Read the story about *Lions* on page 14 of the reading booklet and answer the following questions.

Shade one bubble

1 **The lion is found in ?**
- ○ Africa
- ○ Asia and grassland
- ○ Africa and Asia
- ○ Grassland and Africa

2 **Which sentence is true?**
- ○ Lions are the largest of the big cats
- ○ Lions are the second largest of the big cats
- ○ Lions are the smallest of the big cats
- ○ Lions are not big cats

3 **Which sentence is true?**
- ○ Lions live longer in the wild
- ○ Lions live longer in captivity
- ○ Lions live to the same age in the wild and captivity
- ○ Lions don't live in captivity

4 **The word *pride* could also mean?**
- ○ habit
- ○ hunt
- ○ life
- ○ group

5   **A male lion is recognised by its?**

○ roar

○ size

○ mane

○ tail

6   **Lions hunt in groups for**

○ grass

○ antelope

○ pride

○ fun

Read the story about the *Day at the Park* on page 15 of the reading booklet and answer the following questions

7   **The children want to go to the?**

○ home

○ swings

○ park

○ merry-go-round

8   **The 'she' in line three refers to?**

○ Ben

○ mum

○ Tiffany

○ park

9   **What time does Ben think they have to be home?**

○ two

○ three

○ four

○ five

10 **The word agree can also mean?**

○ allow

○ misuse

○ contend

○ happen

11 **The word *fabulous* can also mean?**

○ mixed

○ fantastic

○ common

○ regards

12 **The phrase *Only if I can have a turn* means?**

○ Tiffany wants to be left at home at the door

○ Tiffany wants to go to the park and play on the swings

○ Tiffany wants to go to the park to play on the merry-go-round

○ Tiffany wants to go to the park until five

Read the story about *Stamp Collecting* on page 16 of the reading booklet and answer the following questions

13 **The best place to find a stamp is on?**

○ a letter

○ an envelope

○ a computer

○ a collector

14 **The world's first stamp was the?**

○ Britain Rose

○ Collector

○ Philatelist

○ Penny Black

15 **A philatelist?**

○ collects stamps

○ studies stamps

○ collects Penny Blacks

○ studies collecting

16 **Which is true?**

○ Stamp collecting is the world's first hobby

○ Stamp collecting is only for children

○ Stamp collecting is one of the world's most popular hobbies

○ Stamp collecting is only for philatelists

17 The word *valuable* in the story could also mean?

○ useless

○ rich

○ delicate

○ expensive

18 Write the numbers 1 to 4 in the spaces to show the order to get a stamp off an envelope

_____ warm some water

_____ peel the stamp off the envelope

_____ dry the stamp on a paper towel

_____ place the stamp and envelope in the water

Read the story about *Anzac Day* on page 17 of the reading booklet and answer the following questions

19 Anzac Day celebrates soldiers from?

○ New Zealand and Turkey

○ Australia and Turkey

○ New Zealand and Australia

○ Turkey and the world

20 **Anzac Day is celebrated every year on the?**

○ 25th April

○ 23rd March

○ 24th April

○ 25th August

21 **Anzacs fought in which country?**

○ England

○ Turkey

○ Australia

○ New Zealand

22 **A Dawn Service would be held in what part of the day?**

○ morning

○ lunchtime

○ afternoon

○ evening

23 **The word *wreath* in the passage is closest in meaning to**

○ a large memorial

○ a present

○ circular decoration of flowers

○ a large signed card

24 **Where are assemblies held to commemorate the day?**

- ⬭ cities
- ⬭ schools
- ⬭ towns
- ⬭ streets

25 **The phrase** *'It is a very important day for all'* **means?**

- ⬭ Anzac Day has great significance
- ⬭ Anzac Day has great monuments
- ⬭ Anzac Day has some memorials
- ⬭ Anzac Day has big celebrations

Read the story about *Kangaroos* **on page 18 of the reading booklet and answer the following questions**

26 **Kangaroos live all over?**

- ⬭ the grasslands
- ⬭ Australia
- ⬭ New South Wales
- ⬭ Western Australia

27 **Male kangaroos are called?**

- ⬭ bucks
- ⬭ joeys
- ⬭ jills
- ⬭ mob

28 **The predators of kangaroos are?**

- ⬭ emus, foxes and goannas
- ⬭ aborigines, eagles and marsupials
- ⬭ dingoes, eagles and goannas
- ⬭ goannas, eagles and emus

29 **The word *kangaroo* is originally a name adapted from?**

- ⬭ explorers
- ⬭ aborigines
- ⬭ Captain James Cook
- ⬭ Australians

30 **Another word for *symbol* in the passage might be?**

- ⬭ money
- ⬭ emblem
- ⬭ show
- ⬭ title

31 **The phrase '*adapted well to human habitation*' means?**

- ⬭ kangaroos live with people as pets
- ⬭ kangaroos have survived despite settlement
- ⬭ kangaroos live poorly with people
- ⬭ kangaroos have survived despite people's pets

Read the story about *The Horseman of Dry Creek* on page 19 of the reading booklet and answer the following questions

32 Abe Finchcombe had always lived at?

○ Dry Creek ranch

○ the Creek

○ Horse River

○ Abe's Place

33 Abe Finchcombe is how old?

○ twenty

○ twenty-one

○ twenty-two

○ twenty-three

34 '*He*' in the line two refers to?

○ Abe's father

○ The horse

○ ranch hands

○ Abe Finchcombe

35 What did Abe's dad warn him about?

○ the hard ground

○ the horse

○ the ranch hands

○ the old wooden fence

36 Another word for *'soothingly'* in the passage might be?

○ calmly

○ roughly

○ raspingly

○ loudly

37 The phrase *'The rangy beast circled around'* means?

○ the horse went wild

○ the horse moved around the yard

○ the horse kicked out at Abe

○ the horse hid spun about

38 Write the numbers 1 to 4 in the spaces to show the order events happen in the story

_____ Abe talked to the horse as he moved closer

_____ Abe drew the horse toward him

_____ Abe walked into the yard

_____ Abe slipped the lead over the horse's head

END OF READING TEST 3

Test 1 Answers

1.   Peter and Jasmine
2.   The children have all day at the circus
3.   clowns
4.   ponies
5.   great
6.   A Day at the Circus
7.   flour and butter
8.   baking powder
9.   1 minute
10. list
11. mixed
12. enjoy
13. February
14. scare off bad luck
15. lantern festival
16. Chinese New Year is not an official holiday in Australia
17. memorable
18. carnival
19. scales
20. laying eggs
21. frog
22. scaly and cold blooded
23. current

24. gecko
25. they live in the rest of the world but not Antarctica
26. fruits, vegetables and nuts
27. she wants to help the environment and save animals
28. they come from animals
29. religion
30. necessary
31. Why I'm a Vegetarian
32. curious
33. castle
34. four
35. stone
36. frightened
37. person
38. Delphi wanders into the castle,
    Delphi slides along the wall,
    Delphi runs for the drawbridge,
    Delphi runs into the iron horse.

Test 2 Answers

1. faithful and loyal
2. Dogs have been with people for centuries
3. guarding, herding and rescue
4. families
5. pull the tail of the dog
6. Man's Best Friend
7. two
8. 50 million
9. Chinese and Japanese
10. joined
11. separate
12. Russia and China
13. four
14. reptiles
15. crocodile
16. Cedric thought the best part of the day was seeing crocodiles
17. tasty
18. to move from side to side
19. Harmony Week
20. food
21. Luigi
22. homemade

23. participation
24. three
25. Carmel enjoyed the dancing
26. patterns of life
27. rainbow
28. orally
29. deepest waterholes
30. gigantic
31. it gives blessings and sickness
32. Akroins
33. sandy and dry
34. Harley and Andy
35. she could defeat them
36. necessary
37. the darkness was all around them
38. Andy and Harley turn to look at their pursuers,
     Andy and Harley head into the tunnels,
     Andy and Harley drive further into the tunnels,
     Andy and Harley see the eyes of an Isikarma.

Test 3 Answers

1. Africa and Asia
2. Lions are the second largest of the big cats
3. Lions live longer in captivity
4. group
5. mane
6. antelope
7. park
8. Tiffany
9. five
10. allow
11. fantastic
12. Tiffany wants to go to the park and play on the swings
13. an envelope
14. Penny Black
15. studies stamps
16. Stamp collecting is one of the world's most popular hobbies
17. expensive
18. warm some water, place the stamp and envelope in the water, peel the stamp off the envelope, dry the stamp on a paper towel
19. New Zealand and Australia

20. 25th April
21. Turkey
22. morning
23. circular decoration of flowers
24. schools
25. Anzac Day has great significance
26. Australia
27. bucks
28. dingoes, eagles and goannas
29. aborigines
30. emblem
31. kangaroos have survived despite settlement
32. Dry Creek ranch
33. twenty-two
34. Abe Finchcombe
35. the horse
36. calmly
37. the horse moved about the yard
38. Abe walked into the yard,
    Abe talked to the horse as he moved closer,
    Abe slipped the lead over the horses head,
    Abe drew the horse toward him